Anonymous

St. John III. - In Most of the Languages and Dialects in which the British and Foreign Bible Society Has Printed or Circulated the Holy Scriptures

Vol. 16

Anonymous

**St. John III. - In Most of the Languages and Dialects in which the British and
Foreign Bible Society Has Printed or Circulated the Holy Scriptures**
Vol. 16

ISBN/EAN: 9783337099732

Printed in Europe, USA, Canada, Australia, Japan

Cover: Foto ©Lupo / pixelio.de

More available books at **www.hansebooks.com**

St. John iii. 16

IN MOST OF THE

LANGUAGES AND DIALECTS

IN WHICH THE

British & Foreign Bible Society

HAS PRINTED OR CIRCULATED THE HOLY SCRIPTURES.

"The Word of THE LORD endureth for ever."

ENLARGED EDITION.

LONDON:

PRINTED FOR THE BRITISH AND FOREIGN BIBLE SOCIETY,

By Gilbert & Rivington, 52, St. John's Square, E.C.

1881.

"FOR GOD SO LOVED THE WORLD,

THAT HE GAVE HIS ONLY BEGOTTEN SON,

THAT WHOSOEVER BELIEVETH IN HIM

SHOULD NOT PERISH,

BUT HAVE EVERLASTING LIFE."

NOTES.

1. The Languages are arranged, as far as practicable, in classes, beginning with those which are simplest in structure, and advancing to the more complex.

2. Where the Society has not translated or published the Gospel according to St. John, a verse is given from some other portion.

3. From this list have been omitted :—

(*a*) Several of the Indian versions, prepared originally by the Serampore Missionaries, but no longer circulated.

(*b*) For the same reason some of the translations made by the first Russian Bible Society.

(*c*) Some of the foreign versions in Roman characters, *e.g.* Norwegian and Swedish.

(*d*) The Society's Scriptures for the Blind in English, Welsh, Arabic, Spanish, &c., as being printed in raised type and on too large a scale to be conveniently represented.

CONTENTS.

A

British & Foreign Bible Society's
SPECIMENS OF LANGUAGES.

◆

I. Isolating (or Monosyllabic) Languages.

1. CHINESE.
(Delegates' Version).

蓋上帝以獨生之子賜世、俾信之者免沈淪、而得永生、其愛世如此。

2. PEKING Mandarin Colloquial.

上帝憐愛世人、甚至將獨生子賜給他們、叫凡信他的不至滅亡、必得永生。

3. NANKING Mandarin Colloq.

上帝把獨生的兒子、賜
給世人、使那信他的人、
免得永遠受苦、可以得
着長久的生命上帝愛
惜世人如此。

4. FOOCHOW Colloq.

耶穌就近來、共伊講天
地隴總其權柄都已經
乞我了。

(*Matt. xxviii. 18.*)

5. SHANGHAE Colloquial.

因為上帝實蓋能愛世界
上個人、直到賞賜自家獨
養個兒子叫勿拘啥人相
信個未勿洛地獄嗒得着
永遠个生命拉、

6. CANTON Colloquial.

因為上帝愛世界甚至
搣佢獨生之子賜過佢
地、令但凡信佢嘅免至
滅亡、又得永生。

7. CANTON Colloquial (*Roman*).

Nó' tsọuṅ, fān, hụ' tọ' ṅo' lọ' tau⸱ ko' šụ', tui khụ' wá⸱ : a' pa,, ṅo' tak, tsuï⸱ thin, kuṅ⸱ a' pa, nì'.
(*Luke* xv. 18.)

8. NINGPO Colloquial (*Roman*).

Ing-we Jing-ming æ-sih shü-kæn-zông zing-ts-ü s-lôh Gyi doh-yiang Ng-ts, s-teh væn-pah siang-sing Gyi cü-kwu feh we mih-diao, tu hao teh-djôh üong-yüu weh-ming.

9. AMOY Colloquial (*Roman*).

Siōng-tè chiong tòk siⁿ ê kiáⁿ hō˙ sè-kan; sìu i ê lâug ⁻m sái tîm-lûu, oē tit-tióh éng oáh; I thià sè-kan án-ni

10. SWATOW Colloquial (*Roman*).   (*Chao-Chow.*)

Uá aiⁿ khí-sin lâi-khụ̀ uá-pẽ--kò, kāng i tàⁿ, Pẽ a, uá tit-tsuẽ--tiéh thiⁿ kuã̄ tõ lụ́ mīu-tsôiⁿ.—(*Luke* xv. 18.)

11. HAKKA Colloquial (*Roman*).   (*Hongkong.*)

Thai'-fam⸱ yu, siu-khu', khai, tšhuṅ,-tam, kai' nyin⸜ hau' loi⸜ tshyu, ṅai⸜, ṅai⸜ pin, ṅi⸜ phiu⸜-ou,.
(*Matt.* xi. 28.)

12. SIAMESE.

เหตุว่าพระเจ้าทรงพระเมตตาความรักษ์ตอมะนุษย์ในโลกย์ เพียงไปรดประทานบิยะบุตรองค์เคียวนั้น มิให้ผู้ใดที่เชื่อในพระองค์นั้นถึงที่นิพหาย

13. BURMESE.

ဘုရားသခင်၌သားတော်ကိုရှိကြဉ်သောသူအပေါင်းတို့သည်ပျက်စီးခြင်းသို့မရောက်။ အစည်ထာဝရအသက်ရှင်ခြင်းကိုရစေခြင်းငှါ ဘုရားသခင်သည်မိမိ၌တပါးတည်းသောသားတော်ကိုစွန့်တော်မူသည်တိုင်အောင်လောကီသားတို့ကိုချစ်သနားတော်မူ၏။

14. BGHAI-KAREN.

တၢ်လၢကစးထးဘဲၣ်လဲးကဆီခဲၢ်ဘဲၣ်နၤက ဒိးဘဲဘဲၣ်သၢဒိ သကၢဝါလီၢ်လဲၢ်လဝးလဲးကဲး ဃၢ, လဲးကဲး တစိကၢဝါလီၢ်လဲၢ်လဝးလဲးပး လဲး,အဖၢးဒၢထူၣ်ရှုးပရုံးလၢ. (1 John i. 3.)

15. SGAU-KAREN.

တၢ်လၢပထံၣ်ဘၣ်, ဒီးပနၢ်ဟူဘၣ်နဲ့ၣ်ပစံး ဘၣ်
တဲဘၣ်၃ ဒီးဒီးၣ်ကၡလိၣ်၃းဒီးပုၢအၢ်လီၢ. ဒီးပ
ဝဲၣ်အၢ်ပၡ လိၣ်ပၢးဒီးပၢ်, ဒီးအၒိၣ်ၢ်ထုၣ်ၡူးပရံး
လီၢ.

(1 *John* i. 3.)

16. PWO-KAREN.

ဘၢ်နိၣ်ၢအၒိၣၡနၣ်၃ၢအဆခၒဟၢ်နိၢ, ဖွဲ့အဟၢ်ထၢဒၢဝ္ၢ
ထခပုၡၢၡအမ္ၢၡ, ဘၢ်အၒိၢဘၢၣ်၃ၢမၡဆခၢ
အၒိၣ်တၣ, ဖိၣ်ၣ်ထၢအၢအၢ့ၣ်၃ၢအဖၢ အိၢ်ဝ္ၢထခမ္ၣ်
၃ၢအဖခၢ်နိၢ်ဆၢ်.

(*Matt.* v. 16.)

17. KHASSI. (*Eastern India.*)

Naba kumta U Blei u la ícit ia ka pyrthei,
katba u la aití-noh ia la U Khún ia u ba-la-
khámarwei, ba uei-uei-ruh u bangeit ha u,
u'n 'nu'm jot shuh, hinrei u'n ioh ka jingim
b'ymjiukut.

18. TIBETAN.

ད་ཀོན་མཚོག་གིས་ཉིད་ཀྱི་སྲས་གཅིག་
པོ་བྱིན་པ་ཙམ་དུ་འཛིག་རྟེན་ལ་བྱམས་
པ་མཛད་དམ། དེ་ལེ་དད་པ་ཐམས་ཅད་
ཉིག་པར་མི་གྱུར་ཀྱི། མཐའ་མེད་པའི་
སྲོག་ཚེབ་པར་བྱའོ॥

19. LEPCHA.

(script)

20. JAPANESE.

ケダシ カミ セケ
ン ヲ カノ ホド ア
イ シテ ソノ ヒト
リ ウマラス ノ ム
スコ ヲ スラ アタ
ヘテ オ ヨソ コレ
ヲ シンズル モノ
ホロバズ シテ カ
ギリ ナキ イノ
チ ヲ エ セシ ム ガ
タメ。

11. AGGLUTINATING LANGUAGES.

1. African.

21. KISWAHELI. (*E. Coast of Africa.*)

Kwani ndivyo Muungu alivyoupenda ulimwengu, akatoa na Mwana wake wa pekee, illi wote wamwaminio waupate uzima wa milele wala wasipotee.

22. KINIKA. (*Wanika Tribes.*)

Niime, nienende kua babayango, ni-mu-ambire, hewe baba, nizikossa hatta uwinguni na emberreso.— (*Luke* xv. 18.)

23. SECHUANA. (*Bechuana Tribes.*)

Gone Morimo o lo oa rata lehatse yalo, ka o lo oa naea Moroa ona eo o tsècoeñ a le esi, gore moñue le moñue eo o rumelañ mo go èna a si ka a hèla, mi a ne le botselo yo bo sa khutleñ.

24. SESUTO. (*Basutoland.*)

Gobane Molimo o ratile lefatsé hakālo, o *le* neile Mora oa oona a tsuetseng a 'notsi; gore e mong le e mong a lumelang go éena, a sé ke a fèla, a mpe a be le bophélo bo sa feleng.

25. KAFIR, or Isixosa.

Ngokuba Utixo walitanda ilizwe kangaka, wada wanika unyana wake okupela kwozelweyo, ukuze osukuba ekolwa kuye angabubi, koko abe nobomi obungunapakade.

26. ZULU. *(South Africa.)*

Kona uTixo wenze njalo wa tanda izwe, we za wa nika indodana yake e zelwe iyodwa, ku te bonke abakolwa iyona ba nga bubi, ba ze ba zuze ukuzwa okunapakade.

27. OTJI-HERERO. *(S. W. Africa.)*

Yehova eye ondyerera n'ombatero yandye, me tira ku ani?: Yehova eye omasa oomuinyo uandye, me urumisiua i ani.—(*Ps.* xxvii. 1.)

28. NAMACQUA. *(Hottentots.)*

‖Natigoseb gom Eloba |hūb-eiba gye lnamo, ob gye ‖c͠ib di |guise |nai hĩ |gõaba gye ma, ‖c͠ib |na ra ‡gomn hoan gä-‖ō tite se, χawen nĩ lamö ũiba ū-ha se.

29. DUALLA. *(Cameroons.)*

Loba lo bo wasi ndulo, na a boli mpom mau mo Muna, na motu na motu nyi dube tenge na mo, a si manyami, 'ndi a ma bene longe la bwindia.

30. HAUSSA. *(Niger.)*

Don Alla ya so dunia hakkanan ši ya bada Dansa nafari, en kowa ya yirda daši, ba ši glata ba, amma ši yi rai hal abbada.

31. IBO. *(Niger.)*

Ma otuáhan Tšúku hónru ēlu'-wana na ánya, ma ya nyére otu oli Opáraya, ma onye owúna kwéreya, ogagi ēfù, ma ga ēwete ndu ēbigebi.

32. NUPÉ. (*Niger.*)

Lugọ ẹbayetinye un nán atši eye ẹzabo, a-a-le etun wanyi 'yeye, a-fe dẑin yebo ndaye nan dan alidẑana nan.—(Matt. v. 16.)

33. YORUBA. (*Slave Coast.*)

Nitori ti Ọlọrun fẹ araiye tobẹ̀ gẹ, ti o fi Ọmọ bíbi rẹ nikanṣoṣo fun ni pe, ẹnikẹni ti o ba gbà a gbọ́ ki yio ṣegbé, ṣugbọn yio ni ìye ti ko nipẹkun.

34. EWE. (*Gold Coast.*)

Ke ši ke nẹnem Mawu elɔ̃a χeχe la me, bena etšo ye ñŭtọ vidšidši deka he na, ne amẹ sya amẹ, si eχo edši ese ko la, mele tšọtšrọ ge wò, nẹkpe wòakpọ agi è mavọ la.

35. ACCRA, or Gã. (*Gold Coast.*)

Ṣi nẹkẹ Nyongmo sumo dṣe lẹ, akẹ e ngô e bi kome, ni a fọ lẹ, e hâ, koni mofẹmo, ni heọ e nô yeọ lẹ, hie a ka kpata, ṣi e na nanô wola.

36. TSCHI, or Twi. (*Gold Coast.*)

Nà sẹnea Onyaṅkōpoṅ dọ w̃iase ni, sẹ ọde ne ba a ọwoo no koro mãe, *na* obiara a ogye no di no anyera, na wanyã dā ṅkwã.

37. MENDE. (*Senegambia.*)

Gbāmailẹ̃ Ngẹ̃wọ iye lọi lo ñi a ndọ̃loi, ta lo i ngi lọi yakpẹ̃i vẹni, iye jọni; ta lo nūmui gbi lo ngi họ̃ua lo a tọ̃nya, ẹ̃ lọ̃hũ, kẹ kūnafo lẹ̃vu lo a jọ.

38. MANDINGO.   (*Senegambia.*)

Katuko Alla ye dunya kannu nyinuyama, an ading wulukilering di, mensating mo-omo men lata ala, ate tinyala, barri asi balu abadaring sotto.

39. BULLOM.   (*Near Sierra Leone.*)

Ntunky kandirr no tre kë aniah ëboll, leh ngha ngha keh mpant no nkeleng, nu kulluh papah no, wonno cheh ko kë foy.—(*Matt.* v. 16.)

40. TEMNE.   (*Near Sierra Leone.*)

Tša yo K'úru ọ poǹ bọ́tạr ara-rū, hā ọ sọnd Ọw'án-k'ọǹ ọ kōm gbo sōn, kǎma w'úni ó w'úni, ọwọ́ láng-kọ, ọ tšē dínng; kẹ́rẹ kǎma ọ sọ́to a-ǹẹ́sạm atabána.

2. Malay, Papuan and Polynesian.

41. MALAGASY.   (*Madagascar.*)

Fa izany no nitiavan' Andriamanitra izao tontolo izao, fa nomeny ny Zanani-lahi-tokana, mba tsy ho very izay rehetra mino Azy, fa hahazo fiainana mandrakizay.

42. NARRINYERI.   (*Australian Aborigines.*)

Lun ellin Jehovah aǹ pornun an Narrinyeri: pempir ile ityan kinauwe Brauwarate, ungunuk korn wurruwarrin ityan, nowaiy el itye moru hellangk, tumbewarrin itye kaldowamp.

43. MALAY.

كرنا دمكين قريس الله سوده مغاسيهي ايسي دنيا
سهيڭݢ كرنياكن انق يڭ توڠݢل سقاي بارڭسياڤ
يڭ ڤرچاي اكن دي تياد اكن بناس هاڽ منداڤت
كهيدوڤن يڭ ككل .

44. MALAY (Roman).

Kŭrna dŭmkianlah halnya Allah tŭlah mŭngasihi
orang isi dunia ini, sahingga dikurniakannya Anak-
nya yang tunggal itu, supaya barang siapa yang
pŭrchaya akan dia tiada iya akan binasa, mŭlainkan
mŭndapat hidop yang kŭkal.

45. LOW MALAY, or Soerabayan. (Batavia.)

Karna sabagitoe sangat Allah soedah mengasehi
isi doenia, sahingga ija soedah membri Anaknja
laki-laki jang toenggal, soepaja sasa-orang jang
pertjaja akan dia, djangan binasa, hanja beroleh
kahidoepan kakal.

46. BATTA (Toba). (Sumatra.)

[Batak script text]

A 3

47. BATTA (Mandaheling) (*Preparing*).

ᯂᯬᯀᯢᯉᯖᯰᯬ᯲ᯖ᯳ᯂᯒᯉᯖᯰ᯲ᯄᯮᯪ᯲ᯀ᯳ᯂ ᯉᯑᯂᯫ᯲ᯖᯬ ᯄᯢᯉ ᯖᯬ. ᯡᯩᯀᯍᯪ ᯀᯬᯡᯪ ᯉᯩᯢᯉ᯳ᯂᯬᯥ ᯀᯒᯖᯰᯬ᯲ ᯂᯬᯪᯢᯉᯖᯰᯬ ᯊᯱᯉ ᯀ ᯖᯬ᯳ᯉ᯴ᯘ ᯖᯬ ᯖᯖᯰᯄᯊᯔ ᯖᯬᯰ᯲ᯗᯱᯘ ᯀᯒ᯳ᯊᯱᯗᯬ ᯖᯬ ᯖᯄ ᯌᯪᯥᯗᯰ ᯂᯬᯤᯬᯌᯰ ᯊᯩᯃᯱ ᯀᯖᯱ ᯌᯒᯬ ᯂᯖ᯳ᯌᯪ᯲ ᯊᯱᯉ ᯀ ᯉᯩ᯳ᯔᯘᯖᯰᯬ᯲ ᯖᯬ ᯖᯰᯂ ᯀᯗᯬᯪᯌᯊᯪ᯲

48. NIAS.   (*Island near Sumatra.*)

Ya'ŏdo edōna máoso ba múido liŏ namāgu, idŏlŏ maṅuá'o liŏṅïa: hē áma! ya'ŏdo hó motōrŏna baliŏ sorūgo, ba fametahóu.—(*Luke* xv. 18.)

49. DYAK, or Dajak.   (*Borneo.*)

Krana kalotä kapaham Hatalla djari sinta kalunen, sampei iä djari menenga Anake idjâ tonggal, nakara gene-genep olo, idjä pertjaja huang iâ, âla binasa, baja mina pambelom awang katatahi.

50. SUNDANESE.   (*Java.*)

Ajeuna mah dek indit ngadeuheusan ka bapa, sarta rek oendjoekan kijeu: Noen ama, simkoering geus tarima migawe dosa ka sawarga sarĕng di pajoeneum ama.—(*Luke* xv. 18.)

51. JAVANESE.

ꦱꦲꦠꦗꦸꦔꦏꦱꦃꦏꦔꦲꦩꦶꦗꦲꦮꦶꦭꦏꦭꦒꦤꦏꦱ꧀ ꦏꦲꦁꦱ꧈ ꦏꦲꦁꦢꦭ꧀ꦥ꧀ꦒꦠꦏꦱꦃꦏꦔꦲꦮꦶꦕꦶꦥ ꧈ꦏꦏꦃꦏꦲꦱꦲꦕꦱꦃꦠꦲꦤꦶꦭꦲꦭꦗꦔꦭꦤꦶꦗꦥꦢ꧀ꦫꦴꦠꦴꦠ꧀ ꧈ꦥꦩꦭꦲꦮꦶꦕꦃꦩꦮꦏꦲꦲꦒꦏꦱꦠꦃꦒꦲꦃꦭꦭ꧈ꦲꦭꦲꦭꦏ ꦏꦲꦱꦏꦭꦏꦸꦗꦶꦔꦤꦶꦭꦴꦫꦴ

52. BALINESE (*Preparing*). (*Bali, Dutch E. Indies.*)

Mapan kèto pitresnan Hida sanghyang Widi tkèn djagaté makedjang, tka Hida nedoenang hokané né sanoenggal kahoetoes mahi, kna Cilang hanaké né ngandelang hi hoka bochoeng naraka, nanging kna hya nepoekin kahidoepan tan pegat.

53. MARÉ, or Nengonese. (*South Seas.*)

Wen' o re naeni Makaze hna raton' o re ten' o re aw, ca ile nubonengo me nunuone te o re Tei nubonengo sa so, thu deko di ma tango ko re ngome me sa ci une du nubon, roi di nubone co numu o re waruma tha thu ase ko.

54. LIFU.

Hna tune la hnimi Cahaze kowe la fene hnengö-drai, mate nyidati a hamane la Nekö i nyidati ka casi, mate tha tro kö a meci la kete i angete lapaune koi nyida, ngo tro ha hetenyi la mele ka tha ase palua kö.

55. IAIAN. (*Uvea.*)

Helang ibetengia anyin Khong ka ang meledran, e ame ham Nokon a khaca thibi, me me ca he ka mok ke at ame labageju kau, kame he ka hu moat ame ca ba balua.

56. ANEITYUMESE.

Is um ucce naiheue vai iji pece asega o Atua is abrai Inhal o un is eti ache aien, va eri eti emesmas a ilpu atimi asgeig iran asega, jam leh nitai umoh irau ineig inyi ti lep ti.

57. EROMANGAN.

Mūve kĭmi, mō mumpi ōvun nūriē cnyx, ōvun numpūn lō sū, wumbaptisō iranda ra nin eni Itemen, ĭm ra nin eni Netni, ĭm ra nin eni Naviat Tumpora.— (*Matt.* xxviii. 19.)

58. FATÉ, or Efatese.

Leatu ki nrum emcromina nin, tewan kin ki tubulua Nain iskeimau i mai, nag sernatamol nag ru seralesok os ruk fo tu mat mou, me ruk fo biatlaka nagmolien nag i tok kai tok mou tok.

59. FIJIAN.

Ni sa lomani ira vaka ko na Kalou na kai vuravura, me solia kina na Luvena e dua bauga sa vakasikavi, me kakua ni rusa ko ira yadua sa vakabauti koya, me ra rawata ga na bula tawa mudu.

60. ROTUMAN.

Ne e fuamamau ne hanis on Oiitu se rantei, ia na on Lee escama, la se raksa teu ne lelea ne maa se ia, la iris po ma ke mauri seesgataaga.

61. TONGAN. (*Friendly Islands.*)

He nae ofa behe ae Otua ki mama ni, naa ne foaki hono Alo be taha nae fakatubu, koeuhi ko ia kotoabe e tui kiate ia ke oua naa auha, kae ma'u ae moui taegata.

62. NIUE, or Savage Island.

Nukua pihia mai e fakaalofa he Atua ke he lalolagi, kua ta mai ai hana Tama fuataha, kia nakai mate taha ne tua kia ia, ka kia moua e ia e moui tukulagi.

63. SAMOAN.

Auā ua faapea lava ona alofa mai o le Atua i le lalolagi, ua ia au mai ai lona Atalii e toatasi, ina ia le fano se tasi e faatuatua ia te ia, a ia maua e ia le ola e faavavau.

64. RAROTONGAN.

I aroa mai te Àtua i to te ao nei, kua tae rava ki te oronga anga mai i tana Tamaiti anau tai, kia kore e mate te akarongo iaia, kia rauka ra te ora mutu kore.

65. MARQUESAN.

Ua kaoha nui mai te Atua i to te aomaama nei, noeia, ua tuu mai oia i taia Tama fanautahi, ia mate koe te enata i haatia ia ia, atia, ia koaa ia ia te pohoe mau ana'tu.

66. TAHITIAN.

I aroha mai te Atua i to te ao, e ua tae roa i te horoa mai i ta'na Tamaiti fanau tahi, ia ore ia pohe te faaroo ia 'na ra, ia roaa râ te ora mure ore.

67. MAORI, or New Zealand.

Na, koia ano te aroha o te Atua ki te ao, homai ana e ia tana Tamaiti ko tahi, kia kahore ai e mate te tangata e whakapono ana ki a ia, engari kia whiwhi ai ki te oranga tonutanga.

3. Dravidian and Kolarian.

68. TAMIL. *(Carnatic and N. Ceylon.)*

தேவன், தம்முடைய ஒரேபேறான குமாரனை விசுவாசிக்கிறவன் எவனோ அவன் கெட்டுப்போகாமல் நித்தியசீவனை அடையும்படிக்கு, அவனைத் தந்தருளி, இவ்வளவாய் உலகத்தில் அன்புகூர்ந்தார்.

69. TELUGU. *(S. E. India.)*

ఎందుకంటే దేవుడు లోకము ప్రేమించుట యేలాగంటే—ఆయన యందు విశ్వాసముంచే ప్రతివాడును నశించక నిత్యజీవము పొందేలాగు తన జనితైక కుమారుని యిచ్చెను.

70. CANARESE. *(Mysore, &c.)*

ಒ೩೦ರೆಂದ೩ ಅವನಲಿ ವಿಶ್ವಾಸವಿಡುವವೆಲ್ಲರು ನಾಶನವಾಗದೆ, ನಿತ್ಯ ಜೀವವನ್ನು ಹೊಂದುವ ಬಗ್ಗೆ, ದೇವರು ಬಬ್ಬನಾಗಿ ಹುಟ್ಟಿದ ತನ್ನ ಮಗನನ್ನು ಕೊಡುವ ಹಾಗೆ, ಲೋಕವನ್ನು ಅಷ್ಟು ಪ್ರೀತಿ ವಾಡಿದನು.

71. MALAYALAM. *(Travancore, &c.)*

എന്തുകൊണ്ടെന്നാൽ ദൈവം തന്റെ ഏകജാതനായ പുത്രനെ, അവനിൽ വിശ്വസിക്കുന്നവൻ ഒരുത്തനും നശിച്ചുപൊകാതെ, നിത്യ ജീവൻ ഉണ്ടാകെണ്ടന്നതിന, തരുവാൻ തക്ക വണ്ണം ഏത്രയും ലൊകത്തെ സ്നെഹിച്ചു.

72. TULU.   (*W. of the Mysore.*)

ದಾಯಿಗಂದಂದಾ ಯಿಡ ನಂಬನಾಯಿ ಯೆಂಗ್ಲ
ನಾಶಿನಾದಮೀಲ್ವಂದಿ ನಿತ್ಯ ಜೀವಯ್ಯುವಾ ಯೆಲಾರ್ದು.
ಮ್ಯುಲೆಶ್ಯದೀಲಿರಿನ ಫ್ಲೊರಿಯಾರ್ದ ಮಟಮುಗನ ಶಾರಿಯೆ.
ಶಿಬಾ ನ್ನಾ್ಲ್ಲ ಶ್ಯಯಿಂಚ್ಸ್ ಪ್ರೀಲಿಮಳ್.

73. GONDI.   (*Central India.*)

स्राहूने मीवा उज्यारो स्रादमीकॅना मुन्ने चमके माई इदेन लिय
कि स्रोके मीवा भलो कानतर हुर्सीकुन मीवोर खर्गवासी दादाना
गुणानुवाद कीर ॥   (*Matt.* v. 16.)

74. SANTALI. (*Bengal Presidency.*)

Nonká báṛe ápe hoṇ hoṛko samáṇgre marsál gṇel
ochoitápe jemon unko hoṇ ápeá: bugi kámi gṇelkáto
áperen sermáren ja:námi: ko sarhauc.—(*Matt.* v. 16.)

75. MONDARI.   (*Koles of Chota Nagpore.*)

चिस्सचि परमेश्वरा मोने लेका सेनतन होड़ो इनीगे स्रइंगा हागा
स्रोड़ो मिस्सी स्रोड़ो स्रइंगा एंगा मेनैया ॥   (*Mark* iii. 35.)

---

4. Hungarian, Finnish and Tartar.

76. HUNGARIAN, or Magyar.

Mert úgy szereté Isten e' világot, hogy az ő
egyetlenegy szülött Fiját adná, hogy minden, valaki
hiszen ő benne, el ne vesszen, hanem örök életet
vegyen.

77. FINNISH.

Sillä niin on Jumala mailmaa rakastanut, että hän andoi hänen ainoan Poikansa, että jokainen kuin uskoo hänen päällensä, ei pidä hukkuman, mutta ijankaikkisen elämän saaman.

78. KARELIAN. (*Finland.*)

Пійнъ ана валгуöвъ шіянъ валгіё пнегмнзіёнъ іёшшя, ю ана няхшяйсь шіянъ гювяшъ азіетъ: и кійшѣшшняйсь шіжнъ Туäшшуö, кумбане онъ шайвагашша. (*Matt.* v. 16.)

79. SAMOGITIAN. (*Wilna.*)

Nesa taipo Diewas numitéjo swieta, jog Sunu sawo wiengimusi báwe : idánt kiekwienas, kurs ing ji tik, ne prazutu, bet turétu amźina giwáta.

80. ESTHONIAN (Dorpat).

Sest nida om Jummal sebba ilma armastanu, et temma omma aino sündinu Poiga om andnu, et kik, kea temma sisse uskwa, hukka ei sa, enge iggawest ello sawa.

81. ESTHONIAN (Reval).

Sest nenda on Jummal ma=ilma armastanud, et temma omma aino siinbinud Poia on annud, et üfkki, kes temma sisse ussub, ei pea hukka jama, waib, et iggawenne ello temmal peab ollema.

82. LAPPONESE.

Jutte nåu etsi Jubmel wáraldeb, atte sodn ulkoswabbi ainarågatum Pardnebs, wai fárt kutte, juffo jakka so nal, i kalka lappot ainat ådtjot ekewen elemeb.

83. RUSS LAPP.

Тэн гудӱк што Иммель пит шабэшііі тан альме, што пджес Альге, эхту-шэнтма эндіи, тэн варас што юкыянъ, Кіе Сонне вісp, ій майкьяхъ, а лехъ сонне агееалмуш.

84 ZIRIAN, or Siryenian. *(Finns about Vologda.)*

Сыдзи медъ югъаллсъ тіанъ югыдъ мортъасъ водзинъ, медъ адзаены тіанлысь бѕpъ керӧмъасъ, и ошклены Ѣатесъ тіанлысь, коды небеслаеъ былынъ.—*(Matt. v. 16.)*

85. WOTJAK *(Preparing).* *(W. Siberia.)*

Озі медъ пиштӧзъ югытъ-тӹ тилядъ адямиӧсъазинъ, сооеъ медъ адзіӧзы дзець уждэеъ тилядъ, сй-но медъ сіотозы Аилы, кудьӹзъ инъ вылыпъ.—*(Matt. v. 16.)*

86. MORDVIN.

Секеъ истя вечкизе Нáзъ масторонь эрицяпъ, мáкеъ мáкеызе цюрапзо сонзé скáмонъ шáчпуманъ, штобы эрьвá кéмиця лáнгозонзо аволь юма, но у́левель пинген ь эрямосо.

87. TCHEREMISSIAN. *(Finns on the Volga.)*

Теньгé яратэиъ Юма сандáликамъ, штá йкъ шкé ӧргажамъ пу́шъ, сáкай пийпыша шы́далапъ йпже-áмъ, а йлеже варá мучáшдэма ку́румъ му́чка.

88. TCHUWASH. *(Volga.)*

Сянлá іӧрáдре Тóра Эдемя, што барзá ху у́вылие перь сюрáдыпие, штобы порь ииляггáнь онá анъ пӥдтаръ, а осрáдаръ іу́мюрьги бу́рпазя.

89. WOGUL *(Preparing).* *(Ural Mountains.)*

Ти-саувт Тӧрим ѣрептистä мерма сто сле-мистä äку-тéлим пувта, исто сокиикар, кон агтта тäве, ат ни колпи, а пора лилма контитä.

A 4

90. ORENBURG, or Kirghise Tartar.

زيراكه خدا جهانني اول قدر سويدي كه بر دوغمش اوغلين بيردي
كه هركيم آنكا ايشانسا هلاى بولمايا لكن ابدي حياتلي بولا ٠

91. TURKISH TARTAR, or Karass. (*Astrakhan.*)

زيرا الله دنيابي شويله سوديكه كندو بريجك اوغلين ويردي تا كه هر كيم
اكا اينانورسه هلاك اولميه اقا ابدي ديرلكي اولا ٠

92. AZERBIJAN, or Transcaucasian Turkish.

زيرا اللّه دنياني ايله سودي كه٠ اوزننك برجه اوغلني ويردي
تا كه هر اونكا ايمان كتورن هـلاك اولمسون بلكه ابدي
حيـاته مـالك اولسون ٠

93. TURKISH.

زيرا الله دنيايى شويله سوديكه هر اكا ايمان ايدن هلاك
اولميوب انجق حيات ابديهيه مـالك اوله ديو كندى
ابن وحيدني اعطا ايلدى ٠

94. GRÆCO-TURKISH.

Ζίρα Ἀλλὰχ τʏνγιαγιὴ πὸυ κατὰρ σεβτί κι, κεντὶ
πιριτζικ Ὀγλουνοῦ βερτὶ, τάκι χὲρ ὀνὰ ἰνανὰν, ζάϊ
ὄλμαγια, ἴλλα ἐπέτι χαϊατὰ μαλὶκ ὀλά.

95. ARMENO-TURKISH.

Օ՛ իրա Լ՛լլա՛հ տիւնեայր պու գատար սեվտի քի`
քէնտի պիրիճիք ()ղլունու վէրտի, թա քի Հէր օնա
ինանան` գայ` օլմայա, իլլա էպէտի Հայաթա մալիք
օլա :

96. MANCHU.

97. MONGOLIAN
Literary.

98. MONGOLIAN
Colloquial.

(Mongolian colloquial script text)

(*Matt.* xxviii. 18.)

99. MONGOLIAN, Buriat
Colloquial.

(Buriat colloquial script text)

100. CALMUC, or Western Mongolian.

5. Basque.

101. FRENCH BASQUE (Labourdin Dialect).

Jaincoac ecen hain maite içan du mundua, non
eman baitu bere Seme bakharra, amorea gatic norc-
ere sinhesten baitu hura baithan gal ez dadin, bainan
çan deçan bethicreco bicia.

102. SPANISH BASQUE.

Alchatuco naiz, eta juango naiz nere aitagana,
eta esango diot: Aita, pecatu eguin nuen ceruaren
contra, eta zure aurrean.—(*Luke* xv. 18.)

103. SPANISH BASQUE (Guipuscoan Dialect).

Joaten ceratela bada eman zayozcatzute eracutsiac jende guciai: batayatzen dituzutela Aitaren, eta Semearen, eta Espiritu santuaren icenean.—(*Matt.* xxviii. 19.)

6. American.

104. ESKIMO.

Taimak Gudib sillaksoarmiut nægligiveit, Ernetuane tunnilugo, illunatik okpertut tapsomunga, assiokonnagit nungusuitomigle innogutekarkovlugit.

105. GREENLAND.

Sillarsúb innue Gudib taima assakigei, Ernetue tunniullugo taukkonunga, tamarmik taursomunga opertut tammarkonnagit, nãksaungitsomigle innursútekarkollugit.

106. TUKUDH. (*Loucheux Indians.*)

Kwugguh yoo Vittukoochanchyo nunh kug kwikyit kettinizhin, tih Tinji chihthlug rzi kwuntlantshị chootyin tte yih kyinjizhit rsyettetgititelya kkwa, kọ sheggu kwundui tettiya.

107. CREE, Eastern (*Syllabic*). (*N. Am. Indians.*)

ᐁᐞᐱᐦᑊ ᒉᔨᐦᕀ ᑭᔭᒉᓄ ᐊᕐᐸᐤ ᕊ ᕀᐤᐅᐞᑊ ᐷᕀ ᐅᐁᔭᐧᓭᖃ , ᐊᐃᕉ ᓂᕷᐧᔪᔥᖃᐧ ᐁᕊ ᐳᕀ ᓂᕐᐊᐧᐁᓂᕐ, ᒐᕊ ᐳᕀ ᐊᕀ ᕊᐸ ᐱᒐᕐᐃᐞ.

108. CREE, Western (*Roman*).

Weya Muneto ā ispeĕche saketâpun uske, kĕ mākew oo pauko-Koosisana, piko una tapwâtowayitche numoweya oo ga nissewunatissĕty, maka oo ga ayâty kakekā pimatissewin.

109. CHIPPEWYAN, or Tinne (*Syllabic*).

ᎣᐅᏬ ᐅᏁᐦᐁ ᒍᓬ ᐁᎢᎢ ᐁᏀᐊᏟ ᐁᏪᔭ ᓓᔑᎢᏁᎢᏬ, ᐁᎢ ᏁᏆᎢ ᐅᏪ ᐁᎳ ᏪᎢᏞᏬ ᎢᎢᎢ ᐁᎢᎢ ᏬᏪ ᓓᎢᏞ ᐊᎢ ᐅᏏᏞ, ᐁᏪᐅᏞᎢ ᐊᏒᏪᎢ ᏪᏬᎢ ᐅᏏᏞ.

110. CHIPPEWYAN, or Tinne (*Roman*).

Apeech zhahwaindung sah Keshamunedoo ewh ahkeh, ooge-oonje megewanun enewh atah tatabenahwa Kahoogwesejin, wagwain dush katapwayainemahgwain chebahnahdezesig, cheahyong dush goo ewh kahkenig pemahtezewin.

111. OJIBWA.

Gaepij shauendk sv rishemanito iu aki, ogionjimigiuenvn iniu etv tibinaue gaoguisijin, aueguen dvsh getebueienimaguen jibvnatizisig, jiaia dvsh go iu kagige bimatiziuin.

112. MALISEET.   (*New Brunswick.*)

Eebŭchŭl Nŭkskam ĕdooche-moosajĭtpŭn ooskĭtkŭmĭkw wĕjemelooĕtpŭn wihwebu Ookwŏŏsŭl, wĕlaman 'mseu wĕn tan wĕlămsŭtŭk oohŭkek, skatŭp ŭksekāhāwe, kānɔokŭloo ooteĭnp askŭmowsooagŭn.

113. MICMAC. (*Indians of Nova Scotia.*)

Mudu Niescąm teliksatcus usitcumu wedji igunum-uedɔgub-unn nɛuktuɪ-bistadjul uewisul, culąmąn m'sit wen tąn kedlamsitc utiɪnincu, mą unmadt jinpuɪc, cądu uscɵtʊ apçuąwɛ miɪmadjuocun.

114. MOHAWK.

Iken ne Yehovah egh ne s'hakonoronghkwa n'ongwe, nene rodewendeghton nene raonhàon rodcwedon rohhàwak, nene onghka kiok teyakaweghdaghkon raonhage yaghten a-onghtonde, ok denghnon aontehodiyendane ne eterna adonhèta.

115. MEXICAN, or Aztec.

Ni mehuaz yhuan ni az campa câ in no tâtzin yhuan nic illhuiz : No tâtzin é, oni tlâtlacô ihuicopa in illhuicatl yhuan mixpan têhuatl.—(*Luke* xv. 18.)

116. MAYAN. (*Yucatan, Central America.*)

Tumen bay tu yacuntah Dioz le yokolcab, ca tu ɔaah u pel mehenan˙˙ Mehen, utial tulacal le max cu yoczietuyol ti leti, ma u kaztal, uama ca yanacti cuxtal minanuxul.

117. AYMARÀ. (*Peru.*)

Hucama Diosaja mundo munana, sapa Yokapa quitani, taque haquenaca iau-siri iñayan hacañapataqui.

7. Caucasus.

118. GEORGIAN (*Civil character*).

რამეთუ ესრეთ შეჰყუარებირა დაჰერთ-
მან სოფელი ესე, ვითარმდეგ ძეცა
თჳსი მაო-ლოო-დ მო-ბიდაი მო-ჰსცა
მას, რათა ფო-გელსა რო-მელსა ჰრ-
წმენეს იგი არა წარჰსწყემდეს, არა-
მედ აქუჰნდეს ცხო-გრება სთჳვჰნო-.

~~~~~~~~~

III. Inflectional Languages.

1. Semitic.

119. HEBREW.

<div dir="rtl">

כי כה אהב אלהים את־העולם כי־נתן את־בנו היחיד ·
למען כל־המאמין בו לא יאבד · כי אם־חיי עולם
יהיו לו :

</div>

120. SYRIAC.

<div dir="rtl">

ܗܟܢܐ ܓܝܪ ܐܚܒ ܐܠܗܐ ܠܥܠܡܐ . ܐܝܟܢܐ
ܕܠܒܪܗ ܝܚܝܕܝܐ ܢܬܠ . ܕܟܠ ܡܢ ܕܡܗܝܡܢ
ܒܗ ܠܐ ܢܐܒܕ . ܐܠܐ ܢܗܘܘܢ ܠܗ ܚܝܐ
ܕܠܥܠܡ .

</div>

121. ARABIC.

لانهُ هكذا احبَّ اللهُ العالَم حتى بذَل ابنهُ الوحيدَ لكي
لا يهلِكَ كلَّ مَن يؤمِن بهِ بل تكون لهُ الحيوةُ الابديَّةُ .

122. JUDÆO-ARABIC. *(Jews in Syria, Yemen, &c.)*

פאנה הכדא יהב אללה אלעאלם חתי בדל אבנה
אלוחיד לכילא יהלך כל מן יומן בה בל יכון לה חיאה
אלאבד :

123. CARSHUN. *(Mesopotamia, &c.)*

[Carshun (Arabic written in Syriac script) text]

124. MALTESE.

Ghaliex Alla hecca hab id dinia illi tâ l'Iben tighu unigenitu, sabiex collmin jemmen bih ma jintilifx, izda icollu il haja ta dejem.

125. ETHIOPIC.

እስመ ፡ ከመዝ ፡ አፍቀሮ ፡ እግዚአብሔር ፡
ለዓለም ፡ እስከ ፡ ወለደ ፡ ዋሕደ ፡ ወሀበ ፡ ቢዛ ፡
ከመ ፡ ኵሉ ፡ ዘየአምን ፡ ቦቱ ፡ ኢይትሐጕል ፡
አላ ፡ ይረክብ ፡ ሕይወተ ፡ ዘለዓለም ።

126. AMHARIC.   (*Abyssinia.*)

እግዚአብሔር ፡ እንዲሁ ፡ ዓለሙን ፡ ወድዋልና ፡
እንድ ፡ ልጁ ን ፡ እስኪሰዉጥ ፡ ድረስ ፡፡ በርሱ ፡
የሞነ ፡ ሁሉ ፡ እንዲደጠፋ ፡ የዘላለም ፡
ሕይወት ፡ ትሆንለት ፡ ዘንድ ፡ እንጅ ፡፡

2. Hamitic.

127. COPTIC.   (*Egypt.*)

Παιρητ ϩαρ ⲁϧϯ ⲙⲉⲛⲣⲉ ⲡⲓⲕⲟⲥⲙⲟⲥ
ϩⲱⲥⲧⲉ ⲡⲉϥϣⲏⲣⲓ ⲙⲙⲁⲩⲁⲧϥ ⲛ̀ⲧⲉϥⲧⲏⲓϥ
ϩⲓⲛⲁ ⲟⲩⲟⲛⲛⲓⲃⲉⲛ ⲉⲑⲛⲁϩϯ ⲉⲣⲟϥ ⲛ̀ⲧⲉϥ-
ϣⲧⲉⲙⲧⲁⲕⲟ ⲁⲗⲗⲁ ⲛ̀ⲧⲉϥϭⲓ ⲛ̀ⲟⲩⲱⲛϧ
ⲛ̀ⲉ̀ⲛⲉϩ.

128. TIGRÉ.   (*Abyssinia.*)

ከምዚውም ፡ ፈትዎ ፡ እግዚአብሔር ፡ ንዓ
ለም ፡ ክሳብ ፡ ዘሀቦ ፡ ብሕቱ ፡ ንዘ ተወለደ ፡
ወዲ ፡ ከይጠፋእ ፡ ኩሌው ፡ ዚአምን ፡
ብኡ ፡ ክትኽነሉ ፡ እምበር ፡ ሕይወት ፡
ዘለዓለም ፡

129. BERBER.   (*N. Africa.*)

مَنَيَّلْ عَلَّمْ كُنْوِ ذَمْوَلَنْ الْهَمْ هَسَنَمْ انتِجكَمْ أَرُو
انُونِ الْمَعْطَ الْعَالِ أَعْفَدْشْ أَمْبَابَهَوْنْ أَقْفِقْنَاوْ
(*Luke* xi. 13.) اَدِفْلَكْ الرَّحْ الْعَالِ إِيَّانْ أَهِتِسْفِسِنْ

130. GALLA.

(South of Abyssinia.)

ዋቃዮን ፡ አካፍቲ ፡ በ.ያ ፡ ለፈ ፡ ዖፈ ፡ ፪ለቲፈ. ፡፡ ኢ.ልዐሣ ፡ ዖፈ ፡ ቶክኝ ፡ ሐሣ ፡ ኺ.ኑ.ቲ ፡፡ ክን ፡ ኢ.ባቲ ፡ አሙኑ ፡ ሁንይ ፡ አካንግኔ ፡፡ ፈዖሣ ፡ በረ. ፡ በረ.ቲ ፡ ኢ.ታ.ቲፈ. ፡ ዐዐሌ ፡፡

131. GALLA (*Roman*).

Waka akana tshalate tshira alami, Umasa tokitsha aka keñe, kan isati amăne aka henbāne, tshenan feia aka tauffe garra duri.

3. Aryan.

a. Indic.

132. SANSKRIT.

ईश्वर इत्थं जगदद्यन यत् स्वमद्वितीयं तनयं प्राददात यतो यः कश्चित् तस्मिन् विश्वसिष्यति सोऽविनाश्यः सन् अनन्तायुः प्राप्स्यति ।

133. SINGHALESE. *(S. Ceylon.)*

මක්නිසාද උබ්වහන්සේ අදහා ගන්නා සිය-ලෙලෝම විනාස නොව සදාකාල ජීවනය ලබනා පිනිස දෙවියන්වහන්සේ තමන්වහන්සේගේ ඒක ජාතපුත්‍රයා දෙවිත් ලොවට දුන්සේක කරුණා කල සේක.

124. PALI. (Ceylon, &c.)

ကသ္သာတံသဒ္ဒုဟ‌‌ၟ‌ဲ၁ သဗ္ဗ အ၀ိၐ္၁ေသတ္ၟ၁
အၐ‌ၟ‌ဲၛိင်ၟဝ‌ံလၐိတ‌ံ ဒေ၀ေါ် သေကၟကၟ္ၟ၁ထ
ပု‌ၟ္ၟ၁ ဒတ္ၟ၁ လောကၟမေတ္တၟကၟပေမၐိ ။

135. PUNJABI, or Sikh.

ਕਿਉਂਕਿ ਪਰਮੇਸਰ ਨੈ ਜਗਤ ਨੂੰ ਅਜਿਹਾ
ਪਿਆਰ ਕੀਤਾ, ਜੋਉਸ ਨੈ ਆਪਲਾ
ਇਕਲੇਤਾ ਪੁਤ੍ਰ ਦਿੱਤਾ; ਤਾਂ ਜਰੇਕ ਜੋ ਉਸ
ਪਰ ਪਤੀਜ, ਤਿਸ ਦਾ ਨਾਸ ਨਾ ਹੋਹੇ, ਸਗਹਾਂ
ਸਦੀਪਰ ਜੀਉਲ ਪਾਹੇ ।

136. MOULTAN, or Wuch, or Ooch.

ᒫᗯᒫᗯ ᠪᐟᕠᠶᐤ ᚇᠵᐤᐁᠶ ᗯᗄ ᠵᕠ ᐸᐤᐸ ᛩᠪ ᛩᠪ ᗯᗄᠵᠤ
ᗯᐱᠵᐳ ᕠᛩ ᕠᐱᛩ ᕠᐟᠵᠤ ᐸᛩ ᛩᠪ ᚦᠶ ᕠᐸᕠᛩ ᗯᐱᠶᠪ ᗯᗄ
ᠪᠪ ᛩᠪᠪᠪᠪ ᛩᕠᛩᕠᠶ ᗯᗄ ᐻᐸ ᠵᠶᚦᠪ ᛩᐸ ᛩᛩ ᛩᠪᠵᠵᠵ ᛩᠪᛩ

137. SINDHI (Arabic). (Western India.)

چا ڪان ت خُداءِ جهان ڪي اِهڙو پيارو رکيو جو پهنّجو
هِڪڙوئي جِطُّلُ پُتُ ڏناءَ ت جيڪوڪو تنہِ تي ويساهُ
آڻي سو جتُ نہ ٿئي ويتر هميشه جِطُّلُ لهي

138. SINDHI (*Gurumukhi character*).

ਫ਼ਾ ਖਾਂ ਉੇਟੋਸੂਰ ਜਰਾਉ ਥੇ ਇਿਹਜ਼ੇ ਪਿਆਰੇ ਰਖੇ ਜੋ ਪਹੰਜੇ
ਹਿਕਿੜੇ ਈ ਜ਼ਲਮਲ ਪੁਟੂ ਡਿਨਾਈਾਂ ਤ ਜੇਰੇ ਰੇ ਉਨਿ ਤੇ ਦੇਮਾਹ
ਆਲੇ ਸੇ ਨਾਸੁ ਨ ਥਿਏ ਵੇਤਰਿ ਮਰਾ ਜਿਝਲ ਲਹੇ ॥

139. HINDI, or Hindui.

क्योंकि ईश्वरने जगतको ऐसा प्यार किया
कि उसने अपना एकलौता पुत्र दिया कि
जो कोई उसपर बिश्वास करे सो नाश न
होय परन्तु अनन्त जीवन पावे ।

140. HINDI (Kaithi).

कयोंकी इसन ने जगत पन ऐसो पनीत की, की उसने अपना
प्रेकलौता पुत्र दीय़ा की जो कोइ उस पन वीसवास लावे सो
नास न होवे पनंतु अनत जीवन पावे ।

141. HINDUSTANI, or Urdu (*Arabic*).

کیونکہ خدا نے دنیا کو ایسا پیار کیا ھی کہ اُسنے اپنا اِکلونا بیٹا دے دیا
تاکہ جو کوئی اُسپر ایمان لاوے ھلاک نہ ہووے بلکہ حیات ابدي پاوے

142. URDU (*Persic*).

کیونکہ خدا نی جہان کو ایسا پیار کیا ہی کہ اُسنے
اپنا اکلوتا بیٹا بخشا تاکہ جو کوئی اُسپر ایمان لاوی
ہلاک نہ ہووی بلکہ ہمیشہ کی زندگی پاوی

143. URDU (*Roman*).

Kyúnki Ḳhudá ne jahán ko aisá piyár kiyá hai, ki us ne apná iklautá Beṭá baḳhshá, táki jo koí us par ímán láwe, halák na ho, balki hamesha kí zindagí páwe.

144. DAKHANI, or Madras Hindustani.

اور خُدا کہا کِہ آسماں کی چوڑاں مَیں روشنیاں ہوویں
کہ دِن کو رات سے جدا کریں اور وے نِشانیوں اور زمانوں
اور دِنوں اور برسوں کے باعِث ہوویں · (.Gen. i. 14)

145. NEPALESE, or Parbutti.

क्याहा ईश्वरले दुनियालाइ एत्तो पियारो गन्या कि उसले आफ्ना एकपैदा होराल्लाइ दियो कि जो हरेक मानिस् उसमाथी विश्वास गर्दछन् सो नाश न होउन् तर अनन्तजिन्दगी पाउन ।

146. BENGALI.

কেননা ঈশ্বর জগতের প্রতি এমত প্রেম করিলেন, যে আপনার অদ্বিতীয় পুত্রকে দান করিলেন ; যেন তাঁহাতে বিশ্বাসকারি প্রত্যেক জন বিনষ্ট না হইয়া অনন্ত জীবন পায় ।

147. BENGALI (*Roman*).

Kenaná Ishwar jagater prati eman dayá karilen, je ápanár adwitíya Putrake pradán karilen ; táháte tánhár bishwáskári pratyek jan nashṭa ná haiyá ananta paramáyu páibe.

148. MUSSULMAN-BENGALI.

সবব খোদা দুনিয়ার তরফে অএশা মেহের করিলন, যে তিনি আপনার একলৌতা বেটাকে বন্শিশ করিলেন, জএশা যে কোন শকশ তাঁহার উপরে ইগান আনে সে হানাক না হইয়া বল্কে হামেশার জেন্দেগি পাইতে পারে ।

149. ASSAMESE.

যি২ মানুহ পুতেকৎ বিশ্বাস কৰে সেই সিবিলাকৰ সৰ্বসাঙ্গ ন হয় কিন্তু অনন্ত আয়ুৰে হয় এই কাৰণ খ্ৰীষ্ট্ৰে আপ্ৰলি অদ্বিতীয় জাত প্ৰক্ৰ দিলে তেঁও এই ৰূপে জগতকে চেনেহ কৰিলে।

150. URIYA. (Orissa.)

ଯେହେତୁ ଭାଗ୍ୟକ୍ରମରେ ପ୍ରତ୍ୟେକ କଣ ବର୍ଷାସକାଶୀ ଯେମନ୍ତ ନଷ୍ଟ ନ ହୋଇ ଅନନ୍ତ ପରମାୟୁ ପାଇବ ଏଥିଁଲାଗି ଇଶ୍ୱର ଜଗତକୁ ଏତେ ପ୍ରେମ କଲେ ଯେ ସେ ଆପଣା ଅଦ୍ୱିତୀୟମ୍ ପୁତ୍ରକୁ ଦେଲେ

151. MARATHI. (Western India.)

कां तर देवाने जगावर एवढी प्रीति केली कीं, त्याने आपला एकुलता पुत्र दिल्हा, यासाठीं कीं जो कोणी त्यावर विश्वास ठेवितो त्याचा नाश होऊं नये, तर त्याला सर्वकालचें जीवन व्हावें.

152. MARATHI (Modi character).

153. GUJARATI. (Western India.)

કેમકે દેવે જગત પર એવડી પ્રીતિ કિધી, કે
તેણે પોતાનો એકાકીજનિત પુત્રએ સારૂ આબો
કે, જે કોઇ તે પર વિશ્વાસ કરે તેનો નાશ ન
થાએ, પણ અનંત જીવન પામે.

154. PARSI-GUJARATI.

કેમકે ખોદાએ દુનીઆ પર એવો પીઆર કીધી
કે તેણે પોતાનો એકાકીજનીત બેટો એ
વાસતે આપીઓ કે, જે કોઇ તેના ઉપર
એતકાદ લાવે તે હલાક ન થાએ, પણ હમેગાંની
ઝંદગી પામે.

155. GITANO. (Spanish Gipsies.)

Mangue ardiñclaré, y chalaré al batusch, y le
penaré: Batu, he querdi crejete contra o Tarpe y an-
glal de tucue.—(*Luke* xv. 18.)

b. Iranic.

156. ARMENIAN (Ancient).

Ո՛ր այնպէս սիրեաց Ասատուած զաշխարհ՝ մինչև
զՈրդին իւր միածին ետ. զի ամենայն որ հաւատայ 'ի
նա՛ մի կորգէ, այլ ընկալցի զկեանն յաւիտենականն.

157. ARMENIAN (Modern).

Ինչու որ Ասատուած անանկ սիրեց աշխարհը, մինչև
որ իր միածին Որդին տուաւ. որ ամէն ով որ անոր
Հաւատայ՝ չկորսուի, հապա յաւիտենական կենքը
ընդունի.

158. ARARAT ARMENIAN.

Պատճառն որ՝ Լ'ստուած եևպես սիրեց աշխարհքին՝ մինչև որ իրան միածին Որդին տուաւ․ որ ամէն ով որ Հաւատայ նորան՝ չըկորչի, այլ յաւիտենական կեանքըն ընդունի:

159. PERSIAN.

زیرا که خدا آنقدر جهان را دوست داشت که فرزند یگانۀ خود را ارزانی فرمود تا که هر کس که بر او ایمان آورد هلاک نشود بلکه زندهگانی جاوید یابد

160. JUDÆO-PERSIC. (*Jews in Persia.*)

זירא כה כדא אן קדר נהאן רא דוסת דאשת כה פרוזנד יכאנה׳ כוד רא ארזאני פרמוד כה תא הר כס כה בר או אימאן אורד הלאך נשוד בלכה זנדגאני נאויד יאבד:

161. OSSETINIAN.　　(*Caucasus.*)

Цæмæйдæріϊтæр Хуцаў афтæ баўарста дунеі, æмæ Jæ jўпæггурϊ Фурϊϊдæр раϊта ўмæп, цæмæj Уj ϊæj ўрпа, ўj ма Фесæфа, фæлæ іп ўа æпусоп царϊ.

162. KURDISH.

Չրիս քո Խոսե վուսան Հուպանա որնե, Հաթա քո եեք ԴՄ Խոսե խո տա, 'Իր Հեր քի քո ժեռա իման սինե վուսա եե պր, լե ժր եպեոի Հայաթա մսէե պրպր:

163. PUSHTOO, or Afghan.

خُلَرَه چَه خُدَاي دنيالره دَارْدنك مِينَه كَرِي
دَه چَه هَغَه خِپِل يُوَه پِيدَا شُوِي زُوِي لره
وركره چَه هَر يُوسِرِي چَه يَهَغَه بَانْد يَقِين
كُوِي هَغَه دهلاك نَشِي لِيكَن بِي‌نهايْته
ژونْدُون دمُومِي *

---

164. ALBANIAN (Tosk).

Σὲ ψὲ Περιτία κάκε ε δέσι πότενε, σὰ κὲ δὰ τὲ πίρρ' ετὶγ
τὲ βέτεμινε, κὲ τζίλι δὸ κὲ τὲ πεσόγε ντὲ αἰ τὲ μὸς χουμπάσε,
πὸ τὲ κέτε γέτεν' ε πὰ σόσουρε

---

165. ALBANIAN (Gheg).

Sepsĕ Perẹndia kaḱi e dešti botẹnẹ, sū δa Bīrin'
e vet, vetẹm-l'ẽminẹ, pẹr mos me uvdierẹ ǵioẹ-kuš
t'i besoyẹ, por tẹ ketẹ yetẹ tẹ pa-sŏsẹme.

---

c Græco-Roman.

166. GREEK.

Οὕτω γὰρ ἠγάπησεν ὁ Θεὸς τὸν κόσμον, ὥστε
τὸν υἱὸν αὐτοῦ τὸν μονογενῆ ἔδωκεν, ἵνα πᾶς ὁ
πιστεύων εἰς αὐτὸν μὴ ἀπόληται, ἀλλ' ἔχῃ ζωὴν
αἰώνιον.

167. MODERN GREEK.

Διότι τόσον ἠγάπησεν ὁ Θεὸς τὸν κόσμον, ὥστε ἔδωκε τὸν Υἱὸν αὐτοῦ τὸν μονογενῆ, διὰ νὰ μὴ ἀπολεσθῇ πᾶς ὁ πιστεύων εἰς αὐτὸν, ἀλλὰ νὰ ἔχῃ ζωὴν αἰώνιον.

168. MODERN GREEK (*Roman*).

Sicothìs thelo ipaghi pros ton patera mu, ke thelo ipì pros afton, Pater, imarton is ton uranou ke enopion su.—(*Luke* xv. 18.)

169. ROUMAN (*Cyril character*).

Къчï аша а iввït Dъmnezeȣ лъmea, къ а дат пе Фïiъл съȣ чел ȣнъłnъскът, ка тот чел че кpede .pn ел съ nȣ пеаръ, чï съ аïбъ вïiаџъ вечnïкъ.

170. ROUMAN (*Roman*).

Caci aşa a iubit Dumueḑeu lumea, încat a dat pre Fiiul seu cel unul-nascut, ca tot cel ce crede in el sî nu se pierḑe, ci sî aiba vieţa eterna.

171. LATIN.

Sic enim Deus dilexit mundum, ut Filium suum unigenitum daret, ut omnis qui credit in eum non pereat, sed habeat vitam eternam.

172. FRENCH.

Car Dieu a tellement aimé le monde, qu'il a donné son Fils unique, afin que quiconque croit en lui ne périsse point, mais qu'il ait la vie éternelle.

173. ITALIAN.

Perciocchè Iddio ha tanto amato il mondo, ch'egli ha dato il suo unigenito Figliuolo, acciocchè chiunque crede in lui non perisca, ma abbia vita eterna.

174 VAUDOIS. *(Waldenses, N. Italy.)*

Perqué Diou ha tant vourgù bén ar mount, qu'a l ha dounà so Fill unic, per que quiounqué cré en el perissé pâ, mà qu'a l abbia la vita étcrnella.

175. PIEDMONTESE.

Përché Iddiou a l ha voulsù tantou ben al mound, ch'a l ha dait so Fieul unic, për chë chiounque a i prësta fede a perissa nen, ma ch'a l abbia la vita eterna.

176. ROMANESE (Oberland).

Parchei Deus ha teniu il mund aschi car, ca el ha dau siu parsulnaschiu figl, par ca scadin, ca crei en el, vomi buc á perder, mo hagi la vita perpetna.

177. ROMANESE (Enghadine).

Perche chia Deis ha taunt amâ 'l muond, ch'el ha dat seis unigenit Filg, aciò chia scodün chi craja in el nun giaja à perder, mo haja vita eterna.

178. CATALAN. *(Eastern Spain.)*

Puix Deu ha amat de tal modo al mon, que ha donat son unigenit Fill, á fi de que tot hom que creu en ell no peresca, ans be tinga la vida eterna.

179. SPANISH.

Porque de tal manera amó Dios al mundo, que ha dado á su Hijo Unigénito, para que todo aquel que en el cree, no se pierda, mas tenga vida eterna.

180. JUDÆO-SPANISH. *(Spanish Jews in Turkey.)*

פורקי אנסי אמו איל דײו אה איל איל מונדו אסטה דאר אה סו איוו
ריגאלאדו פאהרה קי טודו איל קי קרײי אין איל נו סי דיפײידרה
סינו קי טינגה בידה דיː סיײמפרי ·

181. PORTUGUESE.

Porque de tal maneira amou Deus ao mundo, que deu a seu Filho unigenito, para que todo aquelle que n'elle crê, não pereça, mas tenha a vida eterna.

182. INDO-PORTUGUESE. *(Colonies in Ceylon, &c.)*

Parqui assi Deos ja ama o mundo, qui elle ja da sua só gerado Filho, qui quemseja lo cré ne elle nada ser perdido senão qui lo acha vida eterno.

---

d. Celtic.

183. BRETON. *(Brittany.)*

Rag evel-se eo en deus Doue caret ar bed, ma en deus roed e Vab unik-ganet, evit na vezo ket collet pioubenag a gred ennan, mes ma en devezo ar vuez eternel.

184. WELSH.

Canys felly y carodd Duw y byd, fel y rhoddodd efe ei unig-anedig Fab, fel na choller pwy bynnag a gredo ynddo ef, ond caffael o hono fywyd tragywyddol.

185. GAELIC. *(Highlands of Scotland.)*

Oir is ann mar sin a ghràdhaich Dia an saoghal, gu'n d'thug e 'aon-ghin Mhic féin, chum as ge b'e neach a chreideas ann, nach sgriosar e, ach gu'm bi a'bheatha shiorruidh aige.

186. IRISH.

Oịṅ ịṛ ṁaṗ ṛo ṫo ṡṛáòṅ̇ṡ Ḋịa aṅ ṫóṁaṅ, ṡo ṫṫuṡ ṛé a éṁṡeịṅ Ⱥ)ḣeịc ṛéịṅ, ịoṅ̃uṛ ṡịò bé ċṗeịṫeaṛ aṅ̃ ṅ̃aċ ṗaċaò ṛé a ṁũṡa, aċṫ ṡo ṅ̃beịṫ aṅ bẹ̇ṫa ṛịoṗṅ̃ṫe aịṡe.

187. IRISH (*Roman*).

Oír is mar so do ghrádhuigh Día an domhan, go dtug sé a éinghein Meic fein, ionnus gidh bé chreideas ann, nach rachadh sé a mugha, achd go mbeith an bheatha shiorruidhe aige.

188. MANX. *(Isle of Man.)*

Son lheid y ghraih shen hug Jee da'n theihll, dy dug eh e ynrycan Vac v'er ny gheddyn, nagh jinnagh quoi-erbee chredjagh aynsyn cherraghtyn, agh yn vea ta dy bragh farraghtyn y chosney.

e. Scandinavian.

189. ICELANDIC.

Því svo elskaði Guð heiminn, að hann gaf sinn eingetinn Son, til þess að hver, sem á hann trúir, ekki glatist, heldur hafi eilíft líf.

190. NORWEGIAN.

Thi saa haver Gud elsket Verden, at han haver givet sin Søn den eenbaarne, paa det at hver den, som troer paa ham, ikke skal fortabes, men have et evigt Liv.

191. SWEDISH.

Ty så älskade Gud werldena, att han utgaf sin enda Son, på det att hwar och en, som tror på honom, skall icke förgås, utan få ewinnerligit lif.

192. DANISH.

Thi saa haver Gud elsket Verden, at han haver givet sin Søn den eenbaarne, at hver den, som troer paa ham, ikke skal fortabes, men have et evigt Liv.

f. Teutonic.

193. ENGLISH.

For God so loved the world, that he gave his only begotten Son, that whosoever believeth in him should not perish, but have everlasting life.

194. DUTCH.

Want alzoo lief heeft God de wereld gehad, dat Hij zijnen eeniggeboren' Zoon gegeven heeft, opdat een iegelijk, die in Hem gelooft, niet verderve, maar het eeuwige leven hebbe.

195. FLEMISH.

Want alzoo lief heeft God de wereld gehad, dat hij zijnen eeniggeboren Zoon gaf; opdat allen, die in hem gelooven, niet verloren worden, maar het eeuwige leven hebben.

196. NEGRO-ENGLISH.   (*Surinam.*)

Bikasi na so fasi Gado ben lobbi kondre, va a gi da *wan* Pikien va hem, va dem allamal, dissi briebi na hem, no sa go lasi, ma va dem habi da Liebi vo tehgo.

197. GERMAN.

Also hat Gott die Welt geliebet, daß er seinen einge= bornen Sohn gab, auf daß Alle, die an ihn glauben, nicht verloren werden, sondern das ewige Leben haben.

198. JUDÆO-GERMAN. (*Jews in Germany.*)

דען אלזא האט גאט געליבט דיא וועלט געליעבעט, דאס ער וויינען
אייגגעבארנען זאהן גאב, אויך דאס אללע, דיא אן איהן גלויבען, ניכט
פערלאָרען ווערדען, זאנדערן דאז עוויגע לעבען האבען.

199. JUDÆO-POLISH. (*Jews in Poland.*)

וָואֵרִין נָאט הָאט הָאט דִיא וֶועלְט אַזוֹ גֶעלִיבְּט. דָאשׁ עֵר
דָאט גִינֶעבְּין זֵיין אֵיינְצִיגֶען זוּהֶן. אַז אִיטְלִיכֶר וָואשׁ
גְלֵייבְּט אָן אִיהֶם זָאל נִיט פַר־לוֹרִין וֶוערִין. נֵייעֶרְט
עֵר זָאל הָאבִין דָאשׁ אֵייבִּינִי לֶעבִּין:

200. SLAVONIC.

Та́кѡ бо возлюби́ Бг҃ъ мі́ръ, ꙗ́кѡ и҆ Сн҃а своего̀ є҆диноро́днаго да́лъ є҆́сть, да вса́къ вѣ́руѧй въ ѻ҆́нь, не поги́бнетъ, но и҆́мать живо́тъ вѣ́чный.

201. RUSS (Modern).

Ибо такъ возлюбилъ Богъ міръ, что отдалъ Сына своего единороднаго, дабы всякій, вѣрующій въ Него, не погибъ, но имѣлъ жизнь вѣчную.

202. RUTHENIAN. (*Little Russia.*)

Вста́вши по́йдꙋ до ѻ҆тца̀ мо́его, і҆ зка́жꙋ ѥ҆мꙋ̀: Ѻ҆тче, згрѣши́въ ѥ҆м проті́в неба і҆ перед тобо́в.— (*Luke* xv. 18.)

203. BULGARIAN.

За́щото Бог҃ъ толкозь възлюби свѣ́тъ-тъ, щото даде Сы́на своего̀ є҆динороднаго, за да не погыне всакой който вѣрꙋва въ него, но да има животъ вѣченъ.

204. SERVIAN.

Јер Богу тако омиље свијет да је и спна својега јединороднога дао, да ни један који га вјерује не погине, него да има живот вјечни.

205. CROATIAN.

Jer Bogu tako omilje svijet da je i sina svojega jedinorodnoga dao, da ni jedan koji ga vjeruje ne pogine, nego da ima život vječni.

206. SLOVENIAN.

Kajti tako je Bog ljubil svet, da je sina svojega edinorojenega dal, da kdorkoli veruje va-nj, ne pogine, nego da ima večno življenje.

207. BOHEMIAN, or Tsech.

Nebo tak Bůh milowal swět, že Syna sweho gednorozenčho dal, aby každý, ktož wěrj w něho, nezahynul, ale měl žiwot wěcný.

208. POLISH.

Albowiem tak Bog umilowal świat że syna swego iednorodzonego dal, aby każdy, kto weń wierzy, nie zginął, ale miał żywot wieczny.

209. POLISH (*Roman*).

Albowiem tak Bóg umilował świat, że Syna swego iednorodzonego dal, aby każdy, kto weń wierzy, nie zginął, ale miał żywot wieczny.

210. WENDISH (Upper).   (*Lusatia.*)

Pschetoż tak je Boh ton Sswjet lubowal, so won sswojeho jenicżkeho narodżeneho Ssyna dal je, so bychu schitży, kiż do njeho wjerja, shubeni nebyli, ale wjecżne żiwenje mjeli.

211. WENDISH (Lower).   (*Lusatia.*)

Pscheto tak jo Bohg ten sswět lubowal, aż won sswojogo jabnoporojonego ssynna dal jo, abú schykne do niogo wěreze, sgubone ńebuli, ale to ńimerne żůwcńe mějli.

212. HUNGARIAN-WENDISH. (*Wends in Hungary.*)

Ar je tak lübo Bôg ete szvêt, da je Sziná szvojega jedinorodjenoga dáo, dá vszáki, kí vu nyem verje, sze ne szkvarí, nego má 'zítek vekivecsni.

213. LETTISH, or Livonian.

Un tif lohti Deews to pafauli mihlejis, ka winsch sawu pafchu wennpeebsinmufchu Dehlu irr bewis, ka wisseem tcem, kas tizz cekfch winna ne buhs pasustees, bet to muhschigu dsihwofchanu dabbuht.

214. LITHUANIAN.

Taipo Diews mhlejo swieta, kad sawo wiengim=nusi sunu dáwe, jeib wissi i ji tikki ne prapultu, bet amzina ghwata turrétu.

215. PEGUESE. (*Burmah.*)

(*Should follow Burmese, No. 13.*)

(*Gal.* v. 1.)

British & Foreign Bible Society.

THIS Society was instituted in 1804, with the object of circulating the Word of God throughout the world. More than eight and a half millions sterling have been spent by it in the work of translating, revising, printing, and disseminating the Scriptures, and more than eighty-five millions of Bibles, Testaments, and Portions have issued from its depôts, in about two hundred and thirty languages and dialects.

There is hardly a country in the globe which has not felt the influence of this Society. Not only does it possess agents and correspondents, colporteurs and depôts, in every part of Europe, but it is working as the handmaid of all the great Missionary Societies among the most distant nations of the earth. Syrians and Persians, Indians and Chinese, Abyssinians and Kafirs, the islanders of Madagascar, New Zealand and the South Seas, Mexicans and Esquimaux, with many others, can say that through its means they hear in their own tongues the wonderful works of God.

Christian workers of all denominations are cordially invited not only to contribute to the Society's funds, but also to draw from its stores of precious seed. Schools and hospitals, prisons and reformatories, railway-stations and hotels, the army and the navy, can testify to the blessing it has conferred upon them. Poverty, trouble, sickness, and even blindness, present a claim to which it never turns a deaf ear. Public and social movements, emigrations, international exhibitions, wars, fires, floods, are regarded as so many occasions for its renewed exertions, and for the introduction of God's Word into fresh channels.

Whilst adopting standard versions of the Scriptures whenever possible, the Society encourages the formation of new translations both by grants of money and books, and takes every precaution for securing their accuracy. More than two hundred versions of the whole or parts of the Bible have thus been made, many of them in languages which had not previously been reduced to a written form.

The average issues from the London depôt alone are about five thousand volumes a day, and from the various foreign depôts, taken together, the issues are still greater. Printing-presses are employed by the Society, not only in London, Oxford and Cambridge, but also at Paris, Brussels, Amsterdam, Berlin, Cologne, Vienna, Rome, Madrid, Lisbon, Copenhagen, Stockholm, St. Petersburg, Constantinople, Beyrout, Bombay, Madras, Calcutta, Shanghai, Capetown, Sydney, and other centres of activity.

TO GOD BE ALL THE GLORY!

British & Foreign Bible Society.

President—Rt. Hon. the EARL OF SHAFTESBURY, K.G.
Secretaries—Rev. C. JACKSON. Rev. S. B. BERGNE.
Office—146, Queen Victoria Street, London, E.C..

FOREIGN CENTRAL AGENCIES.

FRANCE—M. Gustave Monod, 58, Rue de Clichy, Paris.

BELGIUM—Mr. Kirkpatrick, 5, Rue de la Pépinière, Brussels.

HOLLAND—Mr. H. J. Reesse, Oude Zijds Voorburgwal, K. 157; Amsterdam.

DENMARK—Rev. J. Plenge, Copenhagen.

NORWAY—(Honorary Correspondent) Captain H. M. Jones, V.C., H. B. M. Consul, Christiania.

SWEDEN—(Correspondent) Rev. Dr. Rohtlieb, Stockholm.

GERMANY—Rev. G. Palmer Davies, B. A., 33, Wilhelm. Strasse, Berlin. Also at Frankfort-on-Maine and Cologne.

AUSTRIAN EMPIRE—Mr. Edward Millard, 6, Elisabeth Strasse, Vienna.

ITALY—Mr. T. H. Bruce, 85, Via del Corso, Rome.

SPAIN—Mr. Richard Corfield, 46, Calle de Preciados, Madrid.

PORTUGAL—(Correspondent) Rev. Robert Stewart, Lisbon.

RUSSIA—Rev. W. Nicolson, St. Petersburg (and Moscow); Mr. J. Watt, Odessa (and Tiflis).

TURKISH EMPIRE and GREECE—Rev. Dr. Thomson, Constantinople, Athens and Alexandria.

INDIA—Auxiliary Societies at Bombay, Lahore, Allahabad, Calcutta, Madras, Bangalore, Colombo and Jaffna.

CHINA and JAPAN—Mr. Samuel Dyer, Shanghai and Tokio.

AUSTRALASIA—Rev. J. T. Evans, M.A., Melbourne.—Auxiliaries in Queensland, New South Wales, Victoria, South Australia, Tasmania and New Zealand.

AFRICA—Auxiliaries at Cape Town, Port Elizabeth, Graham's Town, King William's Town, Pietermaritzburg, D'Urban, Lagos, Sierra Leone, Bathurst, &c.

BRITISH NORTH AMERICA — Auxiliaries in Upper and Lower Canada, Nova Scotia, New Brunswick, Prince Edward Island, Newfoundland, &c.

WEST INDIES — Auxiliaries in Bermuda, Jamaica, Antigua, Bahamas, Barbadoes, Dominica, British Guiana, &c.

CENTRAL AND SOUTH AMERICA—Depôts and Agencies in Rio de Janeiro, Buenos Ayres, and Rosario.

www.ingramcontent.com/pod-product-compliance
Lightning Source LLC
Chambersburg PA
CBHW031808090426
42739CB00008B/1210